50 The Best Pies in Town

By: Kelly Johnson

Table of Contents

- Classic Apple Pie
- Cherry Pie
- Pumpkin Pie
- Pecan Pie
- Lemon Meringue Pie
- Key Lime Pie
- Chocolate Cream Pie
- Banana Cream Pie
- Coconut Cream Pie
- Sweet Potato Pie
- Blueberry Pie
- Strawberry Rhubarb Pie
- Peach Pie
- Blackberry Pie
- Raspberry Pie
- Mixed Berry Pie
- Pear Pie
- Plum Pie
- Maple Pecan Pie

- Chess Pie
- Buttermilk Pie
- Cream Cheese Pie
- Silk Pie
- S'mores Pie
- Nutella Pie
- French Silk Pie
- Ice Cream Pie
- Mud Pie
- Mincemeat Pie
- Coconut Custard Pie
- Apple Cranberry Pie
- Lemon Chess Pie
- Cherry Almond Pie
- Chocolate Peanut Butter Pie
- Almond Joy Pie
- Lemon Blueberry Pie
- Bourbon Pecan Pie
- Honey Pie
- Caramel Apple Pie
- Spiced Pear Pie

- Sweet Corn Pie
- Walnut Pie
- Chocolate Cherry Pie
- Raspberry Almond Pie
- Cranberry Orange Pie
- Cranberry Custard Pie
- Grape Pie
- Butter Pecan Pie
- Salted Caramel Apple Pie
- Brown Butter Pecan Pie

Classic Apple Pie

(A timeless favorite with a flaky crust and sweet, spiced apples)

Ingredients:

- 2 1/2 pounds of apples (such as Granny Smith or Honeycrisp), peeled and sliced
- 1 tbsp lemon juice
- 1/2 cup sugar
- 1/2 cup brown sugar
- 1 tsp ground cinnamon
- 1/4 tsp ground nutmeg
- 1 tbsp all-purpose flour
- 1/4 tsp salt
- 2 tbsp butter, cut into small pieces
- 1 package refrigerated pie crusts (or homemade if preferred)

Instructions:

1. **Preheat oven to 425°F (220°C).**
2. **Toss apple slices with lemon juice** in a large bowl. Add sugars, cinnamon, nutmeg, flour, and salt, and stir to combine.
3. **Place one pie crust** in a 9-inch pie pan, then fill it with the apple mixture. Dot the top with butter.
4. **Cover with the second pie crust**, crimping the edges to seal. Cut slits in the top to allow steam to escape.
5. **Bake for 45-50 minutes**, or until the crust is golden and the filling is bubbling.
6. **Cool slightly** before serving. Enjoy!

Cherry Pie

(Sweet and tart cherries wrapped in a buttery crust)

Ingredients:

- 4 cups fresh or frozen cherries (pitted)
- 3/4 cup sugar
- 1/4 cup cornstarch
- 1/4 tsp almond extract
- 1 tbsp lemon juice
- 1 tbsp butter
- 1 package refrigerated pie crusts (or homemade)

Instructions:

1. **Preheat oven to 400°F (200°C).**
2. **In a saucepan, combine cherries, sugar, cornstarch, almond extract, and lemon juice.** Cook over medium heat, stirring constantly, until the mixture thickens.
3. **Remove from heat** and stir in butter.
4. **Place one pie crust** in a 9-inch pie pan, then pour the cherry filling into it.
5. **Top with the second crust**, sealing the edges and cutting slits for steam.
6. **Bake for 45-50 minutes**, until the crust is golden and the filling is bubbly.
7. **Cool before serving.**

Pumpkin Pie

(A creamy, spiced custard pie perfect for fall)

Ingredients:

- 1 can (15 oz) pumpkin puree
- 3/4 cup sugar
- 1/2 tsp ground cinnamon
- 1/4 tsp ground ginger
- 1/4 tsp ground nutmeg
- 1/4 tsp ground cloves
- 2 large eggs
- 1 can (12 oz) evaporated milk
- 1 tsp vanilla extract
- 1 package refrigerated pie crusts (or homemade)

Instructions:

1. **Preheat oven to 425°F (220°C).**
2. **In a large bowl, whisk together the pumpkin, sugar, spices, eggs, evaporated milk, and vanilla.**
3. **Pour the mixture into the prepared pie crust.**
4. **Bake for 15 minutes**, then lower the temperature to 350°F (175°C) and continue baking for 40-45 minutes, or until a knife inserted into the center comes out clean.
5. **Cool completely** before serving.

Pecan Pie

(A rich, sweet pie filled with crunchy pecans)

Ingredients:

- 1 1/2 cups pecan halves
- 1 cup corn syrup
- 3/4 cup sugar
- 1/4 cup melted butter
- 3 large eggs
- 1 tsp vanilla extract
- 1/4 tsp salt
- 1 package refrigerated pie crusts (or homemade)

Instructions:

1. **Preheat oven to 350°F (175°C).**
2. **In a large bowl, whisk together the corn syrup, sugar, melted butter, eggs, vanilla, and salt.**
3. **Place the pecans in the bottom of the prepared pie crust**, then pour the syrup mixture over them.
4. **Bake for 50-60 minutes**, or until the filling is set and slightly golden.
5. **Cool completely** before slicing.

Lemon Meringue Pie

(A tart lemon filling topped with a fluffy meringue)

Ingredients for filling:

- 1 1/2 cups sugar
- 1/4 cup cornstarch
- 1/4 tsp salt
- 1 1/2 cups water
- 3 large egg yolks, lightly beaten
- 1/2 cup fresh lemon juice
- 1 tbsp lemon zest
- 2 tbsp butter

Ingredients for meringue:

- 3 large egg whites
- 1/2 tsp vanilla extract
- 6 tbsp sugar

Instructions:

1. **Preheat oven to 350°F (175°C).**
2. **For the filling:** In a saucepan, whisk together sugar, cornstarch, and salt. Gradually add water and cook over medium heat, stirring constantly, until the mixture thickens.
3. **Stir in the egg yolks** and cook for 2 minutes, then remove from heat and stir in lemon juice, zest, and butter.
4. **For the meringue:** Beat the egg whites until soft peaks form, then gradually add sugar and vanilla, continuing to beat until stiff peaks form.

5. **Pour the lemon filling** into the baked pie crust, then spread the meringue on top, sealing the edges.

6. **Bake for 10-15 minutes**, or until the meringue is golden.

7. **Cool before serving.**

Key Lime Pie

(A refreshing, tangy pie with a graham cracker crust)

Ingredients for filling:

- 3 large egg yolks
- 1 can (14 oz) sweetened condensed milk
- 1/2 cup fresh lime juice
- 2 tsp lime zest

Ingredients for crust:

- 1 1/2 cups graham cracker crumbs
- 1/4 cup sugar
- 1/2 cup butter, melted

Instructions:

1. **Preheat oven to 350°F (175°C).**
2. **For the crust:** Mix the graham cracker crumbs, sugar, and melted butter. Press into the bottom of a 9-inch pie pan.
3. **Bake the crust for 10 minutes**, then cool slightly.
4. **For the filling:** Whisk together the egg yolks, sweetened condensed milk, lime juice, and zest.
5. **Pour the filling into the crust** and bake for 10-12 minutes, or until the filling is set.
6. **Cool completely** before refrigerating for at least 4 hours before serving.

Chocolate Cream Pie

(A smooth, indulgent pie with a chocolate custard filling)

Ingredients for filling:

- 2 cups heavy cream
- 1 cup whole milk
- 3/4 cup sugar
- 1/4 cup cornstarch
- 1/4 tsp salt
- 4 large egg yolks
- 8 oz semisweet chocolate, chopped
- 1 tsp vanilla extract

Ingredients for crust:

- 1 1/2 cups chocolate cookie crumbs
- 1/4 cup sugar
- 1/4 cup butter, melted

Instructions:

1. **Preheat oven to 350°F (175°C).**
2. **For the crust:** Mix the cookie crumbs, sugar, and melted butter. Press into the bottom of a 9-inch pie pan.
3. **Bake for 8-10 minutes**, then cool.
4. **For the filling:** In a saucepan, whisk together cream, milk, sugar, cornstarch, and salt. Cook over medium heat until thickened.

5. **Whisk the egg yolks**, then slowly add the hot mixture, whisking constantly. Return to the heat and cook for another 2 minutes.

6. **Stir in the chocolate and vanilla**, then pour into the prepared crust.

7. **Refrigerate for at least 4 hours** before serving with whipped cream.

Banana Cream Pie

(A creamy, dreamy pie with fresh bananas and a silky custard filling)

Ingredients for filling:

- 2 cups whole milk
- 3/4 cup sugar
- 1/4 cup cornstarch
- 1/4 tsp salt
- 4 large egg yolks
- 2 tbsp butter
- 1 tsp vanilla extract
- 2 bananas, sliced

Ingredients for crust:

- 1 1/2 cups graham cracker crumbs
- 1/4 cup sugar
- 1/2 cup butter, melted

Instructions:

1. **Preheat oven to 350°F (175°C).**
2. **For the crust:** Mix the graham cracker crumbs, sugar, and melted butter. Press into the bottom of a 9-inch pie pan.
3. **Bake for 8-10 minutes**, then cool.
4. **For the filling:** Whisk together the milk, sugar, cornstarch, and salt in a saucepan. Cook over medium heat until thickened.

5. **Whisk the egg yolks**, then slowly add the hot mixture, whisking constantly. Return to the heat and cook for another 2 minutes.

6. **Stir in butter and vanilla**, then pour into the prepared crust.

7. **Top with sliced bananas** and refrigerate until set.

8. **Serve with whipped cream.**

Coconut Cream Pie

(A rich, coconut-filled dessert with a silky custard)

Ingredients for filling:

- 2 cups whole milk
- 3/4 cup sugar
- 1/4 cup cornstarch
- 1/4 tsp salt
- 4 large egg yolks
- 1 cup sweetened shredded coconut
- 2 tbsp butter
- 1 tsp vanilla extract

Ingredients for crust:

- 1 1/2 cups graham cracker crumbs
- 1/4 cup sugar
- 1/2 cup butter, melted

Instructions:

1. **Preheat oven to 350°F (175°C).**
2. **For the crust:** Mix the graham cracker crumbs, sugar, and melted butter. Press into the bottom of a 9-inch pie pan.
3. **Bake for 8-10 minutes**, then cool.
4. **For the filling:** Whisk together the milk, sugar, cornstarch, and salt in a saucepan. Cook over medium heat until thickened.

5. **Whisk the egg yolks**, then slowly add the hot mixture, whisking constantly. Return to the heat and cook for another 2 minutes.

6. **Stir in coconut, butter, and vanilla**, then pour into the prepared crust.

7. **Chill for several hours** and top with whipped cream before serving.

Sweet Potato Pie

(A comforting, spiced pie with a smooth sweet potato filling)

Ingredients:

- 2 cups mashed sweet potatoes (about 2 medium potatoes)
- 1/2 cup sugar
- 1/4 cup brown sugar
- 1/2 tsp cinnamon
- 1/4 tsp nutmeg
- 1/4 tsp ginger
- 1/4 tsp salt
- 2 large eggs
- 1/2 cup evaporated milk
- 1 tsp vanilla extract
- 1 package refrigerated pie crusts (or homemade)

Instructions:

1. **Preheat oven to 350°F (175°C).**
2. **Mash the sweet potatoes** until smooth and mix with sugar, spices, salt, eggs, evaporated milk, and vanilla.
3. **Pour into the prepared pie crust** and bake for 50-60 minutes or until the filling is set.
4. **Cool completely** before serving.

Blueberry Pie

(A sweet and juicy berry pie with a flaky crust)

Ingredients:

- 4 cups fresh or frozen blueberries
- 3/4 cup sugar
- 1/4 cup cornstarch
- 1/4 tsp cinnamon
- 1 tbsp lemon juice
- 1 tbsp butter
- 1 package refrigerated pie crusts (or homemade)

Instructions:

1. **Preheat oven to 400°F (200°C).**
2. **In a saucepan, combine blueberries, sugar, cornstarch, cinnamon, and lemon juice.** Cook over medium heat, stirring constantly, until thickened.
3. **Pour into the prepared pie crust**, then dot with butter.
4. **Top with the second pie crust**, sealing the edges and cutting slits for steam.
5. **Bake for 45-50 minutes**, until the crust is golden and the filling is bubbling.
6. **Cool before serving.**

Strawberry Rhubarb Pie

(A tart and sweet combination of strawberries and rhubarb)

Ingredients:

- 1 pre-made pie crust
- 2 cups fresh strawberries, hulled and sliced
- 2 cups rhubarb, chopped
- 1 1/4 cups sugar
- 2 tbsp cornstarch
- 1 tbsp lemon juice
- 1 tsp vanilla extract

Instructions:

1. **Preheat oven to 375°F (190°C).**
2. **In a bowl, mix strawberries, rhubarb, sugar, cornstarch, lemon juice, and vanilla.**
3. **Pour the mixture into the pie crust.**
4. **Cover with a second pie crust** and seal the edges.
5. **Bake for 45-50 minutes**, until the crust is golden and the filling is bubbly.
6. **Cool before serving.**

Peach Pie

(A sweet and juicy peach pie that's perfect for summer)

Ingredients:

- 1 pre-made pie crust
- 5 cups peeled and sliced peaches
- 1 cup sugar
- 2 tbsp cornstarch
- 1 tbsp lemon juice
- 1/2 tsp ground cinnamon
- 1 tbsp butter

Instructions:

1. **Preheat oven to 375°F (190°C).**
2. **In a bowl, toss peaches with sugar, cornstarch, lemon juice, cinnamon, and butter.**
3. **Pour the mixture into the pie crust** and cover with a second crust.
4. **Bake for 45-50 minutes**, until the crust is golden and the filling is bubbling.
5. **Cool before serving.**

Blackberry Pie

(A fruity and slightly tart blackberry pie)

Ingredients:

- 1 pre-made pie crust
- 5 cups fresh blackberries
- 1 cup sugar
- 1 tbsp lemon juice
- 1/4 cup cornstarch
- 1/4 tsp ground cinnamon
- 1 tbsp butter

Instructions:

1. **Preheat oven to 375°F (190°C).**
2. **In a bowl, mix blackberries, sugar, lemon juice, cornstarch, cinnamon, and butter.**
3. **Pour the mixture into the pie crust** and cover with a second crust.
4. **Bake for 45-50 minutes**, or until the crust is golden and the filling is bubbly.
5. **Cool before serving.**

Raspberry Pie

(A sweet and slightly tart pie with fresh raspberries)

Ingredients:

- 1 pre-made pie crust
- 4 cups fresh raspberries
- 1 cup sugar
- 1 tbsp lemon juice
- 2 tbsp cornstarch
- 1 tbsp butter

Instructions:

1. **Preheat oven to 375°F (190°C).**
2. **In a bowl, toss raspberries with sugar, lemon juice, cornstarch, and butter.**
3. **Pour the mixture into the pie crust** and cover with a second pie crust.
4. **Bake for 40-45 minutes**, or until the crust is golden and the filling is bubbly.
5. **Cool before serving.**

Mixed Berry Pie

(A combination of berries for a vibrant and delicious pie)

Ingredients:

- 1 pre-made pie crust
- 2 cups fresh strawberries, hulled and sliced
- 1 cup blueberries
- 1 cup raspberries
- 1 cup blackberries
- 1 1/2 cups sugar
- 2 tbsp cornstarch
- 1 tbsp lemon juice
- 1/4 tsp ground cinnamon

Instructions:

1. **Preheat oven to 375°F (190°C).**
2. **In a bowl, toss the berries with sugar, cornstarch, lemon juice, and cinnamon.**
3. **Pour the mixture into the pie crust** and cover with a second crust.
4. **Bake for 45-50 minutes**, until the crust is golden and the filling is bubbling.
5. **Cool before serving.**

Pear Pie

(A sweet and fragrant pie made with ripe pears)

Ingredients:

- 1 pre-made pie crust
- 5 cups peeled and sliced pears (preferably Bartlett or Bosc)
- 1 cup sugar
- 1 tbsp lemon juice
- 2 tbsp flour
- 1 tsp ground cinnamon
- 1 tbsp butter

Instructions:

1. **Preheat oven to 375°F (190°C).**
2. **In a bowl, mix pears with sugar, lemon juice, flour, and cinnamon.**
3. **Pour the mixture into the pie crust** and dot with butter.
4. **Cover with a second pie crust** and seal the edges.
5. **Bake for 45-50 minutes**, until the crust is golden and the filling is bubbling.
6. **Cool before serving.**

Plum Pie

(A sweet and slightly tart pie with fresh plums)

Ingredients:

- 1 pre-made pie crust
- 5 cups fresh plums, pitted and sliced
- 1 cup sugar
- 1 tbsp lemon juice
- 1 tbsp cornstarch
- 1/4 tsp ground cinnamon
- 1 tbsp butter

Instructions:

1. **Preheat oven to 375°F (190°C).**
2. **In a bowl, toss plums with sugar, lemon juice, cornstarch, cinnamon, and butter.**
3. **Pour the mixture into the pie crust** and cover with a second pie crust.
4. **Bake for 45-50 minutes**, or until the crust is golden and the filling is bubbly.
5. **Cool before serving.**

Maple Pecan Pie

(A twist on the classic pecan pie with the flavor of maple syrup)

Ingredients:

- 1 pre-made pie crust
- 1 1/2 cups pecans
- 1 cup maple syrup
- 1/4 cup brown sugar
- 1/4 cup butter, melted
- 3 large eggs
- 1 tsp vanilla extract
- 1/4 tsp salt

Instructions:

1. **Preheat oven to 350°F (175°C).**
2. **In a bowl, whisk together maple syrup, brown sugar, butter, eggs, vanilla, and salt.**
3. **Stir in pecans** and pour the mixture into the pie crust.
4. **Bake for 45-50 minutes**, or until the filling is set and golden.
5. **Cool before serving.**

Chess Pie

(A classic Southern pie with a custard-like filling)

Ingredients:

- 1 pre-made pie crust
- 1 1/2 cups sugar
- 1 tbsp cornmeal
- 1 tbsp flour
- 1/4 tsp salt
- 1/2 cup butter, melted
- 3 large eggs
- 1 tbsp vinegar
- 1 tsp vanilla extract

Instructions:

1. **Preheat oven to 350°F (175°C).**
2. **In a bowl, mix sugar, cornmeal, flour, and salt.**
3. **Add melted butter, eggs, vinegar, and vanilla** and whisk until smooth.
4. **Pour the mixture into the pie crust** and bake for 45-50 minutes, until golden and set.
5. **Cool before serving.**

Buttermilk Pie

(A creamy, custard-like pie with a tangy buttermilk filling)

Ingredients:

- 1 cup buttermilk
- 1 1/2 cups sugar
- 1/4 cup butter, melted
- 3 large eggs
- 1 tbsp flour
- 1/4 tsp salt
- 1 tsp vanilla extract
- 1 package refrigerated pie crusts (or homemade)

Instructions:

1. **Preheat oven to 350°F (175°C).**
2. **In a large bowl, whisk together buttermilk, sugar, butter, eggs, flour, salt, and vanilla.**
3. **Pour into the prepared pie crust.**
4. **Bake for 45-50 minutes,** or until the center is set and lightly golden.
5. **Cool before serving.**

Cream Cheese Pie

(A rich, creamy pie with a smooth, tangy filling)

Ingredients for filling:

- 1 package (8 oz) cream cheese, softened
- 1/2 cup powdered sugar
- 1 tsp vanilla extract
- 1 cup heavy cream, whipped
- 1 pre-made graham cracker crust or homemade

Instructions:

1. **In a bowl, beat together the cream cheese, powdered sugar, and vanilla** until smooth.
2. **Fold in the whipped cream** until well combined.
3. **Spoon into the graham cracker crust** and smooth the top.
4. **Refrigerate for at least 4 hours**, or until firm.
5. **Serve chilled.**

Silk Pie

(A velvety, smooth chocolate pie with a rich filling)

Ingredients:

- 1 pre-made chocolate pie crust
- 1 package (8 oz) cream cheese, softened
- 1 1/2 cups heavy cream
- 1 cup powdered sugar
- 1/2 cup cocoa powder
- 1 tsp vanilla extract
- 1/2 cup chocolate chips, melted

Instructions:

1. **In a bowl, beat together cream cheese, powdered sugar, cocoa powder, and vanilla** until smooth.
2. **Whisk in the melted chocolate.**
3. **Fold in the whipped cream** until the mixture is light and airy.
4. **Spoon into the chocolate crust** and smooth the top.
5. **Chill for at least 4 hours** to allow it to set.
6. **Serve chilled.**

S'mores Pie

(A gooey, marshmallow and chocolate-filled pie with a graham cracker crust)

Ingredients for crust:

- 1 1/2 cups graham cracker crumbs
- 1/4 cup sugar
- 1/2 cup butter, melted

Ingredients for filling:

- 1 cup chocolate chips
- 1/2 cup heavy cream
- 2 cups mini marshmallows

Instructions:

1. **Preheat oven to 350°F (175°C).**
2. **For the crust:** Mix graham cracker crumbs, sugar, and melted butter. Press into the bottom of a 9-inch pie pan.
3. **Bake the crust for 8-10 minutes**, then cool.
4. **For the filling:** In a saucepan, heat the heavy cream over low heat. Once hot, pour over chocolate chips and stir until melted.
5. **Pour the chocolate mixture into the cooled crust**.
6. **Top with marshmallows** and bake for 5-7 minutes until they start to brown.
7. **Cool before serving**.

Nutella Pie

(A rich, hazelnut chocolate pie with a silky Nutella filling)

Ingredients:

- 1 pre-made pie crust
- 1 cup Nutella
- 1 package (8 oz) cream cheese, softened
- 1 cup heavy cream
- 1/4 cup powdered sugar
- 1 tsp vanilla extract

Instructions:

1. **In a large bowl, beat together Nutella, cream cheese, powdered sugar, and vanilla** until smooth.
2. **In a separate bowl, whip the heavy cream** until stiff peaks form.
3. **Fold the whipped cream into the Nutella mixture** until well combined.
4. **Spoon into the prepared pie crust** and smooth the top.
5. **Refrigerate for at least 4 hours** until set.
6. **Serve chilled.**

French Silk Pie

(A creamy, chocolate mousse-like pie with a buttery crust)

Ingredients for filling:

- 1/2 cup unsalted butter, softened
- 1 cup sugar
- 3 oz dark chocolate, melted
- 3 large eggs
- 1 tsp vanilla extract
- 1 pre-made graham cracker crust or homemade

Instructions:

1. **In a large bowl, beat the butter and sugar together** until light and fluffy.
2. **Add the melted chocolate and mix until smooth.**
3. **Beat in the eggs, one at a time,** and add the vanilla extract. Continue to beat until the mixture is light and fluffy.
4. **Pour the filling into the pie crust** and smooth the top.
5. **Refrigerate for at least 4 hours** until set.
6. **Serve chilled.**

Ice Cream Pie

(A fun and refreshing dessert with an ice cream base)

Ingredients for crust:

- 1 1/2 cups crushed graham crackers
- 1/4 cup sugar
- 1/2 cup melted butter

Ingredients for filling:

- 1 quart ice cream (any flavor)
- 1 cup chocolate syrup (optional)
- 1/4 cup whipped cream (for topping)

Instructions:

1. **Preheat oven to 350°F (175°C).**
2. **For the crust:** Mix graham cracker crumbs, sugar, and melted butter. Press into the bottom of a pie pan and bake for 8-10 minutes. Cool completely.
3. **For the filling:** Allow ice cream to soften slightly, then spoon it into the cooled crust.
4. **Drizzle chocolate syrup** on top (optional), then freeze until firm.
5. **Top with whipped cream** and serve chilled.

Mud Pie

(A decadent pie with chocolate, coffee, and a crumbly crust)

Ingredients for crust:

- 1 1/2 cups chocolate cookie crumbs
- 1/4 cup sugar
- 1/2 cup butter, melted

Ingredients for filling:

- 1/2 cup brewed coffee, cooled
- 1 cup heavy cream
- 1 cup chocolate chips
- 1/4 cup sugar

Instructions:

1. **Preheat oven to 350°F (175°C).**
2. **For the crust:** Mix the chocolate cookie crumbs, sugar, and melted butter. Press into the bottom of a 9-inch pie pan and bake for 8-10 minutes. Cool.
3. **For the filling:** In a saucepan, combine brewed coffee, sugar, and chocolate chips. Stir over medium heat until the chocolate melts and the mixture thickens.
4. **Pour the filling into the cooled crust** and refrigerate until set, about 4 hours.
5. **Serve chilled.**

Mincemeat Pie

(A traditional, spiced pie with a fruity, savory filling)

Ingredients:

- 2 cups mincemeat filling
- 1 package refrigerated pie crusts (or homemade)

Instructions:

1. **Preheat oven to 425°F (220°C).**
2. **Place one pie crust** in a 9-inch pie pan.
3. **Fill with mincemeat** and top with the second crust, sealing the edges and cutting slits for ventilation.
4. **Bake for 45-50 minutes** until the crust is golden and the filling is bubbly.
5. **Cool before serving.**

Coconut Custard Pie

(A creamy, coconut-filled pie with a smooth custard base)

Ingredients:

- 1 pre-made pie crust
- 1 cup shredded coconut
- 1 1/2 cups heavy cream
- 1/2 cup sugar
- 4 large eggs
- 1 tsp vanilla extract
- 1/2 tsp coconut extract (optional)
- 1/4 tsp salt

Instructions:

1. **Preheat oven to 350°F (175°C).**
2. **In a bowl, whisk together eggs, sugar, vanilla, coconut extract, salt, and heavy cream.**
3. **Stir in shredded coconut** until well combined.
4. **Pour mixture into the pie crust** and bake for 45-50 minutes, or until the center is set and lightly golden.
5. **Cool before serving.**

Apple Cranberry Pie

(A perfect combination of tart cranberries and sweet apples in a flaky crust)

Ingredients:

- 1 pre-made pie crust
- 5 cups peeled and sliced apples (Granny Smith or Honeycrisp)
- 1 cup fresh cranberries
- 1 cup sugar
- 2 tbsp cornstarch
- 1 tsp cinnamon
- 1/2 tsp nutmeg
- 1 tbsp lemon juice
- 1 tbsp butter

Instructions:

1. **Preheat oven to 375°F (190°C).**
2. **In a large bowl, toss apples, cranberries, sugar, cornstarch, cinnamon, nutmeg, and lemon juice.**
3. **Pour the mixture into the pie crust** and dot with butter.
4. **Cover with a second pie crust** and seal the edges, cutting slits in the top to vent.
5. **Bake for 50-55 minutes**, or until the crust is golden and the filling is bubbling.
6. **Cool before serving.**

Lemon Chess Pie

(A tangy, custardy pie with a hint of lemon)

Ingredients:

- 1 pre-made pie crust
- 1 1/2 cups sugar
- 3 tbsp cornmeal
- 1/2 tsp salt
- 1 tbsp lemon zest
- 1/4 cup lemon juice
- 4 large eggs
- 1/2 cup butter, melted
- 1 tsp vanilla extract

Instructions:

1. **Preheat oven to 350°F (175°C).**
2. **In a bowl, whisk together sugar, cornmeal, salt, lemon zest, and lemon juice.**
3. **Add eggs, melted butter, and vanilla, whisking until smooth.**
4. **Pour the mixture into the pie crust** and bake for 45-50 minutes, or until the filling is set and lightly golden.
5. **Cool before serving.**

Cherry Almond Pie

(A sweet, fruity cherry pie with a hint of almond)

Ingredients:

- 1 pre-made pie crust
- 4 cups pitted cherries (fresh or frozen)
- 1 cup sugar
- 2 tbsp cornstarch
- 1 tsp almond extract
- 1 tbsp lemon juice
- 1/2 tsp almond extract (optional for extra flavor)

Instructions:

1. **Preheat oven to 375°F (190°C).**
2. **In a large bowl, mix cherries, sugar, cornstarch, lemon juice, and almond extract.**
3. **Pour the mixture into the pie crust** and top with a second crust or lattice design.
4. **Bake for 50-55 minutes**, until the crust is golden and the filling is bubbly.
5. **Cool before serving.**

Chocolate Peanut Butter Pie

(A creamy, chocolate and peanut butter combination)

Ingredients for crust:

- 1 1/2 cups chocolate cookie crumbs
- 1/4 cup sugar
- 1/2 cup butter, melted

Ingredients for filling:

- 1 cup creamy peanut butter
- 8 oz cream cheese, softened
- 1 cup powdered sugar
- 1/2 cup heavy cream
- 1 tsp vanilla extract
- 1/2 cup chocolate chips, melted

Instructions:

1. **Preheat oven to 350°F (175°C).**
2. **For the crust:** Mix chocolate cookie crumbs, sugar, and melted butter. Press into the bottom of a 9-inch pie pan and bake for 8-10 minutes. Cool.
3. **For the filling:** Beat together peanut butter, cream cheese, powdered sugar, heavy cream, and vanilla until smooth.
4. **Spoon the filling into the cooled crust** and smooth the top.
5. **Pour melted chocolate over the top** and refrigerate for at least 4 hours until set.
6. **Serve chilled.**

Almond Joy Pie

(A delicious combination of chocolate, coconut, and almonds)

Ingredients for crust:

- 1 pre-made graham cracker crust or chocolate cookie crust

Ingredients for filling:

- 1 1/2 cups sweetened shredded coconut
- 1 cup milk chocolate chips
- 1/2 cup chopped almonds
- 1 cup heavy cream
- 1 tbsp powdered sugar
- 1 tsp vanilla extract

Instructions:

1. **Preheat oven to 350°F (175°C).**
2. **For the filling:** In a saucepan, melt chocolate chips with heavy cream and powdered sugar. Stir until smooth.
3. **Stir in shredded coconut and chopped almonds** until well combined.
4. **Pour the mixture into the pie crust** and bake for 25-30 minutes.
5. **Cool before serving.**

Lemon Blueberry Pie

(A sweet and tart pie with fresh blueberries and tangy lemon)

Ingredients:

- 1 pre-made pie crust
- 2 cups fresh blueberries
- 1 cup sugar
- 1 tbsp lemon zest
- 1/4 cup lemon juice
- 1 tbsp cornstarch
- 1/2 tsp cinnamon
- 1 tbsp butter

Instructions:

1. **Preheat oven to 375°F (190°C).**
2. **In a bowl, mix blueberries, sugar, lemon zest, lemon juice, cornstarch, and cinnamon.**
3. **Pour the mixture into the pie crust** and dot with butter.
4. **Cover with a second pie crust** and bake for 45-50 minutes, until the filling is bubbly and the crust is golden.
5. **Cool before serving.**

Bourbon Pecan Pie

(A rich, nutty pie with a hint of bourbon)

Ingredients:

- 1 pre-made pie crust
- 1 1/2 cups pecans
- 1 cup sugar
- 1/4 cup brown sugar
- 1/2 cup corn syrup
- 3 large eggs
- 1/4 cup bourbon
- 1/4 tsp salt
- 1 tsp vanilla extract

Instructions:

1. **Preheat oven to 350°F (175°C).**
2. **In a bowl, whisk together sugar, brown sugar, corn syrup, eggs, bourbon, salt, and vanilla.**
3. **Stir in the pecans** and pour the mixture into the pie crust.
4. **Bake for 50-55 minutes**, or until the filling is set and golden.
5. **Cool before serving.**

Honey Pie

(A simple, sweet pie with a honey-based filling)

Ingredients:

- 1 pre-made pie crust
- 1 cup honey
- 1/2 cup heavy cream
- 1/4 cup butter
- 1/2 cup sugar
- 2 tbsp cornstarch
- 1 tsp vanilla extract
- 2 large eggs

Instructions:

1. **Preheat oven to 350°F (175°C).**
2. **In a bowl, whisk together honey, heavy cream, butter, sugar, cornstarch, vanilla, and eggs until smooth.**
3. **Pour the mixture into the pie crust** and bake for 30-35 minutes, until the center is set.
4. **Cool before serving.**

Caramel Apple Pie

(A sweet, spiced apple pie with a rich caramel filling)

Ingredients:

- 1 pre-made pie crust
- 5 cups sliced apples (Granny Smith or Honeycrisp)
- 1/2 cup sugar
- 1/2 cup caramel sauce
- 1 tsp cinnamon
- 1 tbsp flour
- 1 tbsp lemon juice
- 1 tbsp butter

Instructions:

1. **Preheat oven to 375°F (190°C).**
2. **In a bowl, mix apples, sugar, cinnamon, flour, and lemon juice.**
3. **Pour the mixture into the pie crust** and drizzle with caramel sauce.
4. **Dot with butter** and bake for 50-55 minutes, until the crust is golden and the filling is bubbling.
5. **Cool before serving.**

Spiced Pear Pie

(A cozy pie with the warmth of cinnamon, nutmeg, and pears)

Ingredients:

- 1 pre-made pie crust
- 5 cups peeled and sliced pears (preferably Bartlett or Bosc)
- 1 cup sugar
- 1 tbsp lemon juice
- 1/2 tsp cinnamon
- 1/4 tsp nutmeg
- 2 tbsp cornstarch
- 1 tbsp butter

Instructions:

1. **Preheat oven to 375°F (190°C).**
2. **In a bowl, toss pears with sugar, lemon juice, cinnamon, nutmeg, and cornstarch.**
3. **Pour the mixture into the pie crust** and dot with butter.
4. **Cover with a second pie crust** and seal the edges, cutting slits in the top for ventilation.
5. **Bake for 45-50 minutes** until the crust is golden and the filling is bubbling.
6. **Cool before serving.**

Sweet Corn Pie

(A creamy, custard-like pie with the sweetness of corn)

Ingredients:

- 1 pre-made pie crust
- 2 cups fresh or frozen corn kernels
- 1 cup heavy cream
- 1/2 cup sugar
- 2 large eggs
- 1 tbsp flour
- 1/2 tsp vanilla extract
- Pinch of salt

Instructions:

1. **Preheat oven to 350°F (175°C).**
2. **In a blender or food processor, blend corn, cream, sugar, eggs, flour, vanilla, and salt** until smooth.
3. **Pour the mixture into the pie crust** and bake for 45-50 minutes, until the pie is set and lightly golden on top.
4. **Cool before serving.**

Walnut Pie

(A rich, nutty pie with a caramel-like filling)

Ingredients:

- 1 pre-made pie crust
- 1 1/2 cups chopped walnuts
- 1 cup sugar
- 1/2 cup light corn syrup
- 1/4 cup butter, melted
- 3 large eggs
- 1 tsp vanilla extract
- 1/4 tsp salt

Instructions:

1. **Preheat oven to 350°F (175°C).**
2. **In a bowl, whisk together sugar, corn syrup, butter, eggs, vanilla, and salt.**
3. **Stir in chopped walnuts** and pour the mixture into the pie crust.
4. **Bake for 45-50 minutes**, or until the filling is set and golden.
5. **Cool before serving.**

Chocolate Cherry Pie

(A decadent combination of sweet cherries and rich chocolate)

Ingredients:

- 1 pre-made pie crust
- 2 cups fresh or frozen cherries, pitted
- 1 cup sugar
- 1 tbsp lemon juice
- 1/4 cup cocoa powder
- 2 tbsp cornstarch
- 1/2 cup dark chocolate chips
- 1 tbsp butter

Instructions:

1. **Preheat oven to 375°F (190°C).**
2. **In a bowl, toss cherries with sugar, lemon juice, cocoa powder, and cornstarch.**
3. **Pour the mixture into the pie crust** and sprinkle with chocolate chips and butter.
4. **Cover with a second pie crust** and seal the edges.
5. **Bake for 45-50 minutes**, until the crust is golden and the filling is bubbling.
6. **Cool before serving.**

Raspberry Almond Pie

(A sweet and nutty pie with the vibrant flavor of raspberries)

Ingredients:

- 1 pre-made pie crust
- 2 cups fresh raspberries
- 1/2 cup almond paste
- 1/2 cup sugar
- 1 tbsp lemon juice
- 2 tbsp cornstarch
- 1/4 tsp almond extract
- 1 egg (for egg wash)

Instructions:

1. **Preheat oven to 375°F (190°C).**
2. **In a bowl, mix raspberries, almond paste, sugar, lemon juice, cornstarch, and almond extract.**
3. **Pour the mixture into the pie crust** and cover with a lattice or full crust.
4. **Brush the top crust with an egg wash** (beat the egg with 1 tbsp water) for a golden finish.
5. **Bake for 40-45 minutes**, or until the crust is golden and the filling is bubbling.
6. **Cool before serving.**

Cranberry Orange Pie

(A tart and sweet combination of cranberries and citrus)

Ingredients:

- 1 pre-made pie crust
- 2 cups fresh cranberries
- 1 cup sugar
- 2 tbsp orange juice
- 1 tsp orange zest
- 1/4 tsp ground cinnamon
- 2 tbsp cornstarch

Instructions:

1. **Preheat oven to 375°F (190°C).**
2. **In a bowl, combine cranberries, sugar, orange juice, orange zest, cinnamon, and cornstarch.**
3. **Pour the mixture into the pie crust** and bake for 40-45 minutes, or until the filling is set and the crust is golden.
4. **Cool before serving.**

Cranberry Custard Pie

(A creamy custard pie with tart cranberries)

Ingredients:

- 1 pre-made pie crust
- 2 cups fresh cranberries
- 1 cup sugar
- 1 cup heavy cream
- 3 large eggs
- 1 tsp vanilla extract
- 1 tbsp flour
- Pinch of salt

Instructions:

1. **Preheat oven to 350°F (175°C).**
2. **In a bowl, whisk together sugar, heavy cream, eggs, vanilla, flour, and salt.**
3. **Stir in cranberries** and pour the mixture into the pie crust.
4. **Bake for 40-45 minutes**, until the custard is set and lightly golden on top.
5. **Cool before serving.**

Grape Pie

(A unique pie made with fresh grapes)

Ingredients:

- 1 pre-made pie crust
- 2 cups seedless red or black grapes
- 1 cup sugar
- 2 tbsp cornstarch
- 1 tbsp lemon juice
- 1/4 tsp ground cinnamon

Instructions:

1. **Preheat oven to 375°F (190°C).**
2. **In a bowl, combine grapes, sugar, cornstarch, lemon juice, and cinnamon.**
3. **Pour the mixture into the pie crust** and bake for 40-45 minutes, until the filling is set and the crust is golden.
4. **Cool before serving.**

Butter Pecan Pie

(A sweet, buttery pie with crunchy pecans)

Ingredients:

- 1 pre-made pie crust
- 1 1/2 cups pecans, chopped
- 1 cup sugar
- 1/2 cup butter, melted
- 1/4 cup corn syrup
- 3 large eggs
- 1 tsp vanilla extract
- 1/4 tsp salt

Instructions:

1. **Preheat oven to 350°F (175°C).**
2. **In a bowl, whisk together sugar, melted butter, corn syrup, eggs, vanilla, and salt.**
3. **Stir in pecans** and pour the mixture into the pie crust.
4. **Bake for 45-50 minutes**, or until the filling is set and golden.
5. **Cool before serving.**

Salted Caramel Apple Pie

(A sweet and salty twist on the classic apple pie)

Ingredients:

- 1 pre-made pie crust
- 5 cups peeled and sliced apples (Granny Smith or Honeycrisp)
- 1/2 cup sugar
- 1/4 cup caramel sauce
- 1 tsp cinnamon
- 1 tbsp flour
- 1 tbsp lemon juice
- 1 tsp sea salt

Instructions:

1. **Preheat oven to 375°F (190°C).**
2. **In a bowl, toss apples with sugar, caramel sauce, cinnamon, flour, lemon juice, and sea salt.**
3. **Pour the mixture into the pie crust** and bake for 50-55 minutes, until the crust is golden and the filling is bubbling.
4. **Cool before serving.**

Brown Butter Pecan Pie

(A rich pecan pie with a nutty, caramelized brown butter flavor)

Ingredients:

- 1 pre-made pie crust
- 1 1/2 cups pecans
- 1 cup brown sugar
- 1/4 cup butter, browned
- 1/4 cup corn syrup
- 3 large eggs
- 1 tsp vanilla extract
- 1/4 tsp salt

Instructions:

1. **Preheat oven to 350°F (175°C).**
2. **In a bowl, whisk together brown sugar, browned butter, corn syrup, eggs, vanilla, and salt.**
3. **Stir in pecans** and pour the mixture into the pie crust.
4. **Bake for 45-50 minutes**, or until the filling is set and golden.
5. **Cool before serving.**

www.ingramcontent.com/pod-product-compliance
Lightning Source LLC
LaVergne TN
LVHW061950070526
838199LV00060B/4048